The Green Bananas

For performance fees and enquiries, please contact
steveyoungwork@hotmail.com

The Green Bananas

By Sue Young

Norman, Rupert and Louise all have problems being assertive, especially with certain people in their lives. They decide to go to a behaviour therapist for some assertiveness training. The therapist is determined to help them solve their problems, but events don't turn out according to plan.

Cast

NORMAN : Henpecked husband
DOREEN : Norman's domineering wife
RUPERT : Stressed out theatre director
JEMIMA : Manipulative theatre actress
LOUISE : Bullied Employee
MR.HAINES : Creepy Boss
BRENDA : Assertiveness Therapist

In this one act play, all characters have a flexible age range.
There are four scenes, a living room, an office, a canteen and a stage. This play had been successfully performed with a minimalist set.
It was performed by the Lancastrian Players in 2013 and enjoyed a successful run, breaking the record for highest box office takings in the history of the company.

SCENE 1

(ENTER NORMAN WITH A CUP OF TEA. HE SITS DOWN AND STARTS WATCHING THE SNOOKER)

DOREEN: (OFFSTAGE) Norman! (NORMAN PANICS AND SPILLS HIS TEA. HE TRIES TO TIDY UP, WIPE THE SPILL ETC. ENTER DOREEN). I hope you're not watching the snooker.

NORMAN: Of course not dear.

DOREEN: If I find that you were watching the snooker, you know what I'll do, don't you?

NORMAN: Yes dear.

DOREEN: I will not tolerate such a silly game in my house.

NORMAN: But it's not a silly game.

DOREEN: What did you say?

NORMAN: Nothing dear.

DOREEN: Snooker is just a couple of grown men in penguin suits, poking a ball around with a long stick.

NORMAN If you say so.

DOREEN: I do. (SNIFFS AIR) It smells like a toilet in here. (SHE PICKS UP AN AIR FRESHENER AND BEGINS TO SPRAY THE ROOM. SHE SPRAYS NORMAN TOO).

NORMAN: (COUGHS AND SPLUTTERS): Did you enjoy yourself at the overnight flower arranging class dear?

DOREEN : What did you say?

NORMAN: I said did you enjoy-

DOREEN: I heard what you said. You've always been sarcastic. Mother was right about you.

NORMAN: But I only asked.

DOREEN: Mr. Thomas and I have a good teacher/student relationship. We're just friends, that's all.

NORMAN: You and Mr Thomas are friends?

DOREEN: Are you accusing me of something?

NORMAN: Certainly not dear.

DOREEN: (PUTS HER COAT ON) Good. Now get this mess cleaned up. .

NORMAN: Where are you going?

DOREEN: I'm going to see...a neighbour.

NORMAN: Which one?

DOREEN: Er...Mrs. Jones across the road. We'll have a natter and a cup of tea...or two, so don't expect me back for a couple of hours. (TAKES A MIRROR FROM HER BAG AND CHECKS HER HAIR AND MAKE UP) Well, don't just stand there. Get this place cleaned up. (NORMAN PRETENDS TO CLEAN UP AN ALREADY TIDY ROOM. EXIT

DOREEN: (OFFSTAGE): And don't forget to mend the garden gate!

NORMAN: (FRANTICALLY, TO HIMSELF): Toolbox...toolbox...must get my toolbox.

(EXIT NORMAN)

SCENE 2

(ENTER RUPERT. HE LOOKS AT HIS WATCH AND PACES THE FLOOR).

RUPERT: She's late...again! All the other actors have gone home because they were tired of waiting for her. Fine. See if I care. What if it's lunchtime? Do I feel stressed? Do I look stressed? No. I'm perfectly calm. I'm perfectly... (TAKES A DEEP BREATH) calm. (HE PAUSES THEN SCREAMS): Where is she? (ENTER JEMIMA) Hello Jemima.

JEMIMA: Darling!

RUPERT: Darling! What happened? Did you sleep in again?

JEMIMA: No, Fluffy the goldfish snuffed it. I had to do the right thing by it and give it a decent burial.

RUPERT: Oh, you poor thing. You must be grieving.

JEMIMA:I am. Could you get me a glass of water for my pills?

RUPERT: If anyone needs a pill it's me. (HE GIVES HER A BOTTLE OF MINERAL WATER AND SHE SWALLOWS HER PILLS) Okay, now, can we get started? Time is money, Jemima.

JEMIMA: Oh yes, of course.

RUPERT: (CLAPS HANDS) Chop! Chop! Let's take it from the top.

JEMIMA: Oh Rupey. You can't expect me to get straight into this thing. I've only just come in.

RUPERT: I have noticed.

JEMIMA: I'm not a machine you know. I need time. I need a warm up.

RUPERT: Okay, fine. Everything stops for Jemima and her own special warm up.

(JEMIMA INDULGES IN A WEAK PHYSICAL WARM UP THAT LASTS TEN SECONDS OR SO, BUT SHE IS OUT OF BREATH BY THE END OF IT). Toned up enough?

JEMIMA: Yes thank you Rupey.

RUPERT: My name is Rupert. Please don't call me Rupey.

JEMIMA: Sorry Rupey.

RUPERT: (PAUSE) Can we get on?

JEMIMA: Er...yes...what scene are we doing?

RUPERT: Scene One of course. We have only just started rehearsing.

JEMIMA: Yes. Of course, how silly of me. (THEY BOTH LAUGH).

RUPERT: Right. Now, pretend your husband has come in. He's been out all night and he's drunk. You've been waiting up for him. Here he comes now...action !

JEMIMA: (VERY FLATLY) Your dinner's in the dog.

RUPERT: Stop !

JEMIMA: What's wrong?

RUPERT: Anger darling...where's the anger?

JEMIMA: Well, I don't show my anger. I introvert it.

RUPERT: Jemima, my little ray of sunshine, this is the acting profession. We pretend. We show our anger. We extrovert it.

JEMIMA: There's no need to get stroppy with me Rupey.

RUPERT: I am not getting stroppy and for the last time will you stop calling me Rupey? Do it again. Take Two.

JEMIMA: Your dinner's in the dog ! (SHE LASHES OUT AT HIM) I hate you ! I hate you!

RUPERT: (HOLDING HER BACK): That's a little bit too much anger darling. Try it again, a bit gentler this time. Take three.

JEMIMA: Your dinner is in the chihauhau.

RUPERT: Stop ! What are you doing?

JEMIMA: I was improvising. I thought it sounded better.

RUPERT: You thought it sounded better ?

JEMIMA: Yes. I'm quite happy with it.

RUPERT: You are? (JEMIMA NODS FERVENTLY) Well, that's interesting because I'm not !

JEMIMA: There's no need to shout.

RUPERT: I'm shouting because I have to shout, because I have lost my temper and because I feel (BREAKS DOWN) very, very angry.

JEMIMA: But why Rupey?

RUPERT: (PAUSE. THEN EXPLODES): It's Rupert!

JEMIMA: I'm sorry.

RUPERT: And it's not Doberman Pinscher, it's not Alsation, it's not Poodle and it's not Chihauhau. It's dog. D-O-G – Dog. Got that?

JEMIMA: Yes.

RUPERT: Good. Take Four.

JEMIMA: (CLEARS THROAT): Your dinner's in the- Oh, no! I've just realised, I'm meeting my sister for lunch today, must dash, see you later. (EXIT JEMIMA)

RUPERT: I think I'll go and have a lie down.

(EXIT RUPERT)

SCENE 3

(ENTER MR. HAINES)

MR. HAINES : (SITS DOWN AT A DESK AND STARTS TO WRITE. HE HEARS A KNOCK ON THE DOOR).Come in.(ENTER LOUISE) Ah, there you. (PAUSE) Well, don't just stand there Louise. Come in, sit down. (LOUISE PULLS UP A CHAIR AND SITS DOWN OPPOSITE MR. HAINES. HE LOOKS UP) How long have you been with this company now?

LOUISE: Er...about a year and a half.

MR. HAINES: Do you enjoy your job?

LOUISE: Oh yes, I love it.

MR. HAINES: But I see that you have applied for a more senior position on the second floor. Why would you want to change your job if you love it?

LOUISE: Well, the promotion comes with a higher salary, better prospects and I'd quite like to better myself I suppose, set some more challenges.

MR. HAINES: Indeed. Do you remember the last office party we had?

LOUISE: Er...no, not really.

MR. HAINES: It was the usual thing, loud music, silly behaviour,
 lots of alcohol flowing...

LOUISE:I think I remember.

MR. HAINES : If I recall, I asked you for a dance?

LOUISE: Did you?

MR. HAINES: And you said you had to be going. It was all very sudden. You'd consumed a little alcohol, so you couldn't drive home and you'd missed the last bus. So I asked you if you'd like a lift home. As I recall it was a quite a cordial invitation.

LOUISE: Oh yes, I remember now.

MR. HAINES: But you refused my kind offer and you have continued to refuse my offers of a lift home ever since.

LOUISE: I'm sorry Mr. Haines. I didn't mean to offend you.

MR. HAINES: But you have offended me Louise.

LOUISE: Like I said, I'm sorry. I don't know what else to say.

MR. HAINES: I can't fault you on your work. You're very good at your job, but not very good at being nice to me. (HE WALKS AROUND THE DESK AND STANDS BEHIND HER) I can honestly say that's something you're not too hot at. (HE LEANS OVER HER AND PICKS UP AN

APPLICATION FORM FROM THE DESK) This is your application for the job upstairs. Mr. Johnson thought it was very impressive, but I told him I didn't think you were ready.

LOUISE: What?

MR. HAINES: Well, every time I extend a hand to you, you bite it off. I don't think you're sociable enough for the second floor. I think you need to work on your people skills. (HE RIPS UP THE APPLICATION IN FRONT OF HER)

LOUISE:(GASPS) But...you can't do that, that's not fair.

MR. HAINES: Life isn't. (HE CONTINUES WRITING. LOUISE STAYS SEATED) Oh, are you still here? Don't you have work to do?

(LOUISE EXITS)

SCENE 4

(ENTER BRENDA, ALONG WITH NORMAN. RUPERT AND LOUISE)

BRENDA: Please sit down and make yourself comfortable. Thank you for coming to my assertiveness training class. My name is Dr. Williams, but I'd like everyone to call me Brenda. Hello everyone.

NORMAN: Hello Brenda.

RUPERT: Hello Brenda.

LOUISE: Hello Brenda.

BRENDA: And your names are?

NORMAN: (QUIETLY) Norman.

RUPERT: I'm Rupert.

LOUISE: (VERY QUIETLY) Louise.

BRENDA: So it's Norman, Rupert, and Louise, wonderful. Just to clarify, I specialise in behaviour therapy. Behaviour therapy consists of three parts: applied behaviour analysis, cognitive behaviour therapy and habit reversal training. Applied behaviour analysis focuses on operant conditioning in the form of positive reinforcement to modify behaviour. Cognitive behaviour therapy focuses on the thoughts and feelings behind mental health conditions and finally, habit reversal training uses treatment plans to decrease habit-like behaviours. Any questions?

(RUPERT RAISES HIS HAND)

BRENDA: Yes Rupert?

RUPERT: Could you tell us what that means in laymen's terms?

BRENDA: Oh yes, sorry, it means you are all doormats and I'm going to put a stop to it. Now, Norman, let's start with you first. Tell us a little bit about yourself. (PAUSE) Whenever you're ready Norman.

NORMAN: I like snooker and...I'm married.

LOUISE: (QUIETLY) I work for an accountancy firm.

BRENDA: Could you speak up please?

LOUISE: I work for an accountancy firm.

RUPERT: I'm a theatre director.

BRENDA: Sounds like an interesting job.

RUPERT: It is very rewarding...normally.

BRENDA: Normally? So you're saying it isn't rewarding now?

RUPERT: Well, no. It's a bit embarrassing actually.

BRENDA: That's all right. I'm here to help you. I won't laugh.

RUPERT: I never said it was funny, just embarrassing.

BRENDA: If you tell me what it is, it won't be embarrassing any more.

RUPERT: It's my first time as a director and my actors are so temperamental. They just won't listen to me, especially Jemima. She's the most difficult of all. I don't think I can cope.

BRENDA: Have you considered dropping her from the cast?

RUPERT: Good lord, no. Her brother owns the theatre...and is funding the play...and is paying my wages.

BRENDA: I see. Well, what's the alternative?

RUPERT: (ANGRILY) There is none. That's why I've come to you.

BRENDA: What I'm sensing here, is an issue with anger. Tell me Rupert,do you get angry, lose control and then get nothing done?

RUPERT: Sometimes.

BRENDA: It seems to me that if you can stand up to Jemima without becoming angry, you'll be able to manage the situation more effectively. Let's start off with some anger management exercises. Stand up. Now what I want you to do is take a deep breath. (HE TAKES A DEEP BREATH) Count to ten slowly.

RUPERT: One...two...

BRENDA: No, not out loud, in your head. You don't want everyone to know you're counting do you?

RUPERT: Oh. (HE CLOSES HIS EYES AND COUNTS IN HIS HEAD)

BRENDA: Okay, take another deep breath. Now, do you feel any better?

RUPERT: I'm not sure. I'm a bit light headed.

BRENDA: Try using visualisation. First, think of all the bad things that might happen if you are aggressive instead of assertive. For instance, the show will probably bomb. You'll be panned in all the art reviews and your career will go down the drain.

RUPERT: Really? How awful.

BRENDA: Then think of all the good things that might happen if you are assertive instead of aggressive. You might get such a good performance from your actors, you could be next year's 'Theatre Director Of the Year.' The way you handle Jemima could be the difference between a smash hit and a flop.

RUPERT: 'Director Of The Year' you say?

BRENDA: That's right. It's all in your hands Rupert. You need to set boundaries. Next time she plays up say, 'I am the director and you are the actress. Explain your different roles. Let her know who's boss.

RUPERT: I'll try.

(NORMAN GETS UP TO LEAVE)

BRENDA: Norman, where are you going?

NORMAN: I...I want to go.

BRENDA: Go where?

NORMAN: Home.

BRENDA: Why?

NORMAN: I'm getting nervous.

BRENDA: It's perfectly okay to be nervous...and leaving a place where you don't want to be is assertive.

NORMAN: Is it?

BRENDA: It is.

NORMAN: Well then, can I go?

BRENDA: You can go if you want to, but it would be better if you stayed. If you didn't want a problem sorting out, you wouldn't be here in the first place would you?

NORMAN: I know but I have to go shopping with my wife now.

BRENDA: Do you always go shopping with your wife?

NORMAN: Yes.

BRENDA: Do you like shopping?

NORMAN: Yes. (LOOKS ABOUT HIM, AS IF SOMEBODY MIGHT BE LISTENING) Well, actually, no, not really. I would like to watch snooker or play it at the local hall but there's no time. I'm always fixing things around the house or doing the dishes or making Doreen a cup of tea.

BRENDA: And Doreen is your wife?

NORMAN: Yes.

BRENDA: And you love her very much?

NORMAN: What kind of a question is that? Yes, of course I love her. (PAUSE) I have to go.

BRENDA: Norman...

NORMAN: I have to do the shopping but I'll be back next week. (TO HIMSELF): Do I love my wife? What a ridiculous question. (EXIT NORMAN)

BRENDA: And what about you Louise? Why have you joined this course?

LOUISE: I have an annoying boss.

BRENDA: Well that's a common problem. What does he do to annoy you?

LOUISE: Everything. He's...creepy.

BRENDA: Oh, that kind of boss. Do you want to tell me more?

LOUISE: No.

BRENDA: No?

LOUISE: Oh, but I will, next time. It's just...I have to go to work right now.

RUPERT: Do accountants work in the evenings?
(EXIT LOUISE)You're frightening them off very well.
BRENDA: Oh, what a disaster!
RUPERT: But I' m still here.
BRENDA: I know. Now remember, stay positive.
RUPERT: You should talk.

(EXIT BRENDA AND RUPERT).

SCENE 5

(ENTER DOREEN. ENTER NORMAN. HE IS WEIGHED DOWN WITH SHOPPING BAGS).

DOREEN: Norman!

NORMAN: Yes dear.

DOREEN: What are you doing?

NORMAN: I'm about to sit down.

DOREEN: I know you're about to sit down, but why? (NORMAN SITS DOWN HEAVILY) Well that was a waste of time because you're going to have to get up now.

NORMAN: Why?

DOREEN: To put all the shopping back and to mend the garden gate.

NORMAN: But I mended the garden gate the other day.

DOREEN: No, you haven't. It's wonky. You need to take it off again and put it on straight.

(EXIT NORMAN) Wait! Come back! (ENTER NORMAN) Where are you going?

NORMAN: To fix the gate.

DOREEN: Make me a cup of tea first. (EXIT NORMAN) Norman! (ENTER NORMAN) Shopping!

(NORMAN RETRIEVES THE SHOPPING AND EXITS AGAIN)

NORMAN: (OFFSTAGE): Do you want cake with your tea dear?

DOREEN: I always have cake.

NORMAN: Oh dear ! Oh no!

DOREEN: Norman? What have you broken? (EXIT DOREEN) (OFFSTAGE) My best china!

NORMAN: (OFFSTAGE) It was an accident.

DOREEN: I'll show you an accident.

NORMAN: Ow! Ouch!

DOREEN: Now that was an accident.

(ENTER DOREEN AND NORMAN. NORMAN IS HOLDING HIS ARM. DOREEN PUTS HER HAND OUT).

NORMAN: What are you doing?

DOREEN: What does it look like?

NORMAN: (HE PUTS HIS HAND IN HIS POCKET AND GIVES HER SOME MONEY)

DOREEN: (LOOKS AT IT) Norman.

NORMAN: Here, take it all. (HE GIVES HER HIS WALLET. EXIT NORMAN. DOREEN MAKES A PHONE CALL ON HER MOBILE)
DOREEN: Hello? Peter? I've just come into some money. How about going for a meal tonight, my treat? (PAUSE) Good. We'll meet at seven thirty, at our usual spot. See you there. Bye.

(EXIT DOREEN)

SCENE 6

(ENTER RUPERT)

RUPERT: What did I expect? Did I expect her to be early? Today, I've got to show her who's boss. Oh no, I'm talking to myself again.
(ENTER JEMIMA WITH A CARRIER BAG FROM A BOUTIQUE)
JEMIMA: That's a sign of madness you know Rupey?
RUPERT: Oh Jemima, you're here at last. Where have you been?
JEMIMA: I've been shopping.
RUPERT: I can see that.
JEMIMA: (JEMIMA TAKES THE DRESS OUT OF THE BAG AND HOLDS IT NEXT TO HER). Do you think it's sexy?
RUPERT: Jemima please. We're running late. We must get on.
JEMIMA: You keep saying that but we've got plenty of time.
RUPERT: No, we haven't. We're still on Scene 1. Jemima? Jemima are you listening to me? (HE GRABS THE DRESS FROM HER AND THROWS IT TO THE FLOOR.
JEMIMA: Oh, how could you? Really Rupey, I don't know what's got into you lately. (RETRIEVES THE DRESS): You're turning into a nasty man. I can't work with you while you're being so nasty.
RUPERT: Now look, your scenes are the only ones in the play left to do. All the others are getting fed up with you. Nathan, Hannah and Matthew have all expressed their exasperation at having to wait around for you.
JEMIMA: Well, where are they now?
RUPERT: They've been here since nine o'clock this morning. I had to send them home.
JEMIMA: Well I'm here now aren't I? Better late than never. We can start rehearsing right now.
RUPERT: Do you have a script?
JEMIMA: I don't need one. I know all my lines.
RUPERT: Oh well then, I'll play Nathan's part. I'll just erm...stand here. Right, are you ready?
JEMIMA: Ready.
RUPERT: Of you go then.
JEMIMA: Your dinner's in the dog.
RUPERT: I'm not very hungry anyway.
JEMIMA: Why did you stay out Jonathan?
RUPERT: I was drowning my sorrows Lizzie.

JEMIMA: Whatever for?

RUPERT: It's because of you Lizzie. I feel as if our relationship is going down the pan. I feel as if every day we're getting further apart from each other, emotionally, spiritually and...physically.

JEMIMA: Oh Jonathan....I'm sorry Rupey. This isn't working.

RUPERT: Why not? I thought it was okay.

JEMIMA: Well, I'm not happy with it. After all, you're not Nathan. At some point I'm going to have to do this scene with him.

RUPERT: Yes, but Nathan's not here.

JEMIMA: I know but you're the director. You should be over there, watching my performance and I'll pretend that Nathan is here. That way you can watch the scene objectively.

RUPERT: Yes of course. We'll try it and see if it works.

JEMIMA: You read Nathan's part.

RUPERT: I feel as if every day we're getting further apart, emotionally, spiritually, physically.

JEMIMA: Oh Jonathan...(SHE EMBRACES THEAIR AND KISSES IT NOISILY) I love you so much. (PAUSE) Well? What do you think Rupey?

RUPERT: I expect it'll be all right on the night.

JEMIMA: What do you mean?

RUPERT: I'm saying it doesn't work for me.

JEMIMA: Well, it's not easy trying to act with the invisible man.

RUPERT: But it was your idea for me to be over here while you're over there!

JEMIMA: Don't shout at me Rupert!

RUPERT: You called me Rupert!

JEMIMA: Yes, I called you Rupert because I'm annoyed with you. Quite frankly, I'm fed up with you shouting at me all the time. I resign. (EXIT JEMIMA)

RUPERT: What? I didn't mean to shout. I was only joking. Come back!

(EXIT RUPERT)

SCENE 7

(ENTER MR. HAINES WHO SITS DOWN. ENTER LOUISE. SHE
PUTS A REPORT ON HIS DESK. SHE IS ABOUT TO EXIT)

MR. HAINES: Er...Louise? Come back here please. Sit down. Now, what
is this thing you've put on my desk?
LOUISE: It's the report you wanted.
MR HAINES: I wanted that report in yesterday.
LOUISE: You said you wanted it in by today.
MR. HAINES: Are you calling me a liar?
LOUISE: No. I wouldn't...
MR. HAINES: (LEANS BACK IN HIS CHAIR) You seem very uptight
Louise.
LOUISE: I'm fine.
MR. HAINES: Do I mind if I ask you a personal question?
LOUISE: Yes.
MR. HAINES: I'll ask it anyway. Do you have a boyfriend?
LOUISE: Yes.
MR. HAINES: Are you sure?
LOUISE: Of course I'm sure. Look, I have to get back to work.
MR. HAINES: Let's call it quits.
LOUISE: What do you mean?
MR. HAINES: Don't be such a sour puss. Let's shake and make up. (HE
PUTS OUT HIS HAND) Come on, I won't bite. (SHE SHAKES HIS
HAND AND TRIES TO PULL AWAY BUT HE PULLS HER TOWARDS
HIM) If you do have a boyfriend, I bet he isn't a gentleman, like I am. I bet
he doesn't do this. (HE KISSES THE BACK OF HER HAND)
LOUISE: I have to get back to work.

(EXIT LOUISE)

SCENE 8

(ENTER NORMAN, RUPERT AND BRENDA)

BRENDA: Now we've had a few meetings and you've told me a bit more about your problems. So I think it's time we got down to some real therapy. Maybe we should have a cup of tea first.

RUPERT: I fancy one myself.

BRENDA: Put the kettle on Norman.(HE GETS UP) Norman, sit down.

NORMAN: But you told me to put the kettle on.

BRENDA: Yes I did, but you don't have to do everything everyone tells you. You have rights.

NORMAN: Rights?

BRENDA: And your rights entitle you to say no to Doreen once in a while.

NORMAN: That's impossible.

BRENDA: Now we're going to do a bit of role playing. Norman, I'm going to pretend to be your wife.

NORMAN: Oh no.

BRENDA: Make a cup of tea Norman.

(EXIT NORMAN)

BRENDA: Norman, where are you going?

(ENTER NORMAN)

NORMAN: You just told me to make some tea again.

BRENDA: But we were role playing.

RUPERT: Is that fruit there for any specific reason?

BRENDA: What?

RUPERT: The fruit on the table? I haven't had much to eat today. May I have a banana?

BRENDA: Yes of course, whatever you want. (RUPERT RUMMAGES AMONG THE FRUIT) Now Norman, let's try again.

RUPERT: (PICKS OUT A GREEN BANANA): All the bananas are green.

BRENDA: Well then, they're as green as you two. Maybe they need to ripen before they get any good.

RUPERT: There's a ripe one here somewhere. (HE FINDS AND PEELS A RIPE BANANA)

BRENDA: Now where was I?

RUPERT: You said you were going to be his wife.

BRENDA: Oh yes, thank you Rupert.

RUPERT: Can I be his wife?

BRENDA: What?

RUPERT: May I play the wife role? I am an actor you know. Well I used to be.

BRENDA: I thought it might be better with me being a woman?

NORMAN: You look nothing like Doreen.

BRENDA: Well Rupert hardly looks like her either.

NORMAN: Oh I don't know, there is some resemblance.

RUPERT: I'm not sure how to take that.

BRENDA: Okay Rupert, if you want to play his wife then do so, but you must ask the right questions.

RUPERT: Oh I will. (WOMAN'S VOICE) Norman, you are a horrible little man. I think we should have separate beds. (HE BITES INTO THE BANANA)

NORMAN: We've already got separate beds and I have to make the beds and fix fences and tidy up. I also have to make her a cup of tea every time she asks for it.

BRENDA: Next time she asks you to do something that you think is unreasonable, you must stand up for yourself and say no Doreen.

NORMAN: Say no Doreen.

BRENDA: No, just say no.

NORMAN: No.

BRENDA: That's it. It's very simple isn't it?

NORMAN: I can say it to you, but she always says to me, 'You know what will happen if you don't do what I want you to do.'

BRENDA: Which is?

NORMAN: You know it's funny, I don't even know what it is that will happen to me, if I don't do what she says.

BRENDA: So, what are you afraid of?

NORMAN: I don't know.

BRENDA: Then it's obviously an idle threat to make you do what she wants. Okay, let's try it with this cup of tea thing. Rupert, please be quiet while I do this. (RUPERT IS INDIGNANT) Norman, make the tea. (PAUSE) What are you waiting for?

NORMAN: I...er...

BRENDA: Are you defying me Norman?

NORMAN: Yes, er...no...oh dear.

BRENDA: Make the tea Norman! You know what will happen if you don't! Tell her no Norman, say it loud and mean it.

NORMAN: I will not make the tea ! I will not make the tea!

BRENDA: Very good. Excellent. Did that make you feel better?

NORMAN: Yes. It make me feel great.

BRENDA: That's because you were being assertive. Next time, say it to your wife and you'll feel like a new man.

NORMAN: A new man?

RUPERT: I wish I was a new man.

BRENDA: Rupert, how are you getting on with Jemima?

RUPERT: She walked out on me in the middle of rehearsals. She resigned.

BRENDA: What are you going to do about the play?

RUPERT: I don't know and I don't care. Actually, she resigns all the time. She'll probably come in tomorrow. She always does... well...eventually.

(ENTER LOUISE)

BRENDA: Oh hello Louise.

NORMAN: Hello Louise.

RUPERT: Hello Louise.

LOUISE: Sorry I'm late.

BRENDA: Take a seat. Don't worry, you haven't missed much. Although Norman is on the way to becoming a new man.

NORMAN: I think my wife's having an affair.

BRENDA: What makes you think that?

NORMAN: It was something she said. She gets on very well with Mr. Thomas. I can't imagine what he sees in her. She's got a voice like a fog horn.

BRENDA: What do you think she sees in him?

NORMAN: I don't know.

BRENDA: Do you really want to be more like Mr. Thomas?

NORMAN: Yes. No. Oh, I don't know!

RUPERT: It sounds like they deserve each other, this Mr. Thomas and your wife. You should leave her.

BRENDA: Rupert!

NORMAN: No. He's right! It has crossed my mind, but what other woman would want me? I'm a weak fool. I'm a mouse.

BRENDA: Stop being a mouse then.

RUPERT: Yes, be more like a gerbil.

BRENDA: Rupert, you're as bad as Norman.

RUPERT: Oh, thank you very much.

BRENDA: Now listen, there's a method that's used in behaviour therapy called 'hierarchy.' You begin by role playing with someone who you don't feel threatened by, and then you step it up, until you finally confront the person who threatens you most. Louise, would you like to role play with Rupert?

LOUISE: I don't know how.

BRENDA: It's quite simple. You just pretend to be Jemima.

RUPERT: There's nothing simple about that.

BRENDA: Louise, tell him you're not rehearsing this week. Go on.

LOUISE: Er...Rupert. I can't rehearse this week.

RUPERT: Why not?

BRENDA: Tell him that you have a migraine. One that will last all week.

RUPERT: Yes, that's exactly the kind of thing she would say.

LOUISE: Rupert, I have a migraine. One that will last all week.

RUPERT: Could you be a bit more squeaky? Jemima can be very high pitched. At least that's how she sounds to me.

LOUISE; (HIGH PITCHED) I can't rehearse because I have a migraine.

RUPERT: Well, you have to rehearse. We're all depending on you.

LOUISE :Oh, okay then.

RUPERT: It's no good. She's useless.

BRENDA: Rupert, that wasn't very nice.

RUPERT: I know I'm sorry Louise. It's just that you could never be Jemima. You're too sweet.

BRENDA: Okay, okay, let's leave it there for now. Next time, we'll work a bit more on NORMAN. Louise, would you stay for a moment please. I think we need a woman to woman chat, just us two. The nature of your problem is...a bit delicate.

LOUISE: You can say that again.

BRENDA: Pick up the banana skin on the way out please Rupert.

(RUPERT PICKS UP THE BANANA SKIN AND EXITS WITH NORMAN).

SCENE 9

BRENDA: You need to tell Mr. Haines that his behaviour is wrong. Tell him if he doesn't stop, you'll go to his boss.

LOUISE: Oh, I don't know. What if he doesn't believe me?

BRENDA: You could take legal action.

LOUISE: Oh, I don't want to do that either. He'll just twist everything, make it sound like it was my fault.

BRENDA: This is why the victim never retaliates and the bully get away with murder. Again, think of the alternative? What is the alternative for you Louise?

LOUISE: I'll leave the company and won't have a job.

BRENDA: So if you don't stand up for yourself, the outcome is worse. You have nothing to lose.

LOUISE: I'm a bit quieter than the other girls in the office. He only ever seems to pick on me. It must be my fault.

BRENDA: It's not your fault. Don't ever think that. Jemima may be a pain in the backside and Norman's wife, well, she's just Norman's wife, but Mr. Haines, I'd really like to sort him out. So, we have no option but to catch him out. (PRODUCES A DICTOPHONE/ RECORDING DEVICE). Now, take this into work, hide it and next time he starts playing his games, press record.

(LOUISE TAKES THE DEVICE AND THEY BOTH EXIT)

SCENE 10

(ENTER NORMAN. HE SITS DOWN, PICKS UP THE PAPER AND STARTS READING).

DOREEN: (OFFSTAGE): Norman! (NORMAN JUMPS AT HER VOICE. ENTER DOREEN) Where's my cup of tea?
NORMAN: What?
DOREEN: I have one at this time every evening.
NORMAN: I was told I couldn't.
DOREEN: What?
NORMAN: My therapist told me not to.
DOREEN: What are you blabbering on about?
NORMAN: Er...nothing.
DOREEN: (PAUSE) Well?
NORMAN: Well what?
DOREEN: Don't just sit there. Why are you so slow witted today?
NORMAN: I...I don't know.
DOREEN: Make-me-some-tea! (EXIT NORMAN) And don't forget to draw fresh water from the tap.
NORMAN: (OFFSTAGE): Yes dear.
DOREEN: And remember I take two sugars now.
NORMAN: (OFFSTAGE): Yes dear.
DOREEN: And just a touch of milk. You always put too much milk in.
NORMAN: Yes. I remember.
(ENTER NORMAN WITH A CUP OF TEA. HE SITS DOWN CALMLY AND SIPS IT. DOREEN GIVES HIM A LONG STARE). Is there something wrong dear?
DOREEN: Where's my tea?
NORMAN: I didn't make you one.
DOREEN: You didn't make me one. Give me that! (GRABS TEA FROM NORMAN AND DRINKS SOME) No sugar and too much milk. Get out into the kitchen and make me a cup of tea. You know what will happen if you don't. (PAUSE) Do it! Now!
NORMAN: (NORMAN GETS UP, IS ABOUT TO EXIT BUT HESITATES)What will happen if I don't make the tea?
DOREEN: How dare you.
NORMAN: I only asked.
DOREEN: Look, forget the tea. I've got better things to do with my time,

than argue with you. I'm going out to my flower arranging class. Don't wait up for me.

NORMAN: You're seeing Mr. Thomas?

DOREEN: (PAUSE) Yes. I am. (EXIT DOREEN)

NORMAN: (STANDS THERE WITH THE CUP OF TEA IN HIS HAND) I wonder what Mr. Thomas does that makes my wife respect him? I bet he stands up straight and doesn't slouch like I do. I bet he's tall, dark and handsome...and smokes a cigar. He'll be strong, deep voiced, commanding...Doreen, I order you....Doreen, I command you... Oh, it's no good. I could never be like that. (DRINKS TEA) Too much sugar.

(EXIT NORMAN)

SCENE 11

(ENTER JEMIMA AND RUPERT)

JEMIMA: Perhaps I was a bit hasty.

RUPERT: Yes, I think you were.

JEMIMA: You know how feisty I get sometimes. Can I have my job back?

RUPERT: I'm not sure. You did resign.

JEMIMA: Oh Rupey, please...pretty please. Pretty, pretty, pretty please.

RUPERT: No.

JEMIMA: But I promise to be good. I'll spend the whole day acting my heart out.

RUPERT: Well...I don't know...the whole day?

JEMIMA: The whole week.

RUPERT: Steady on !

JEMIMA: I mean it Rupey. I'll work right through the week.

RUPERT: And no drinking...no late nights?

JEMIMA: Oh darling, I'm not sure if I can give up my drinking.

RUPERT: And no shopping sprees.

JEMIMA: Mmm....you drive a hard bargain. Maybe you could let me have one drink and one shopping spree?

RUPERT: As long as you're in early every morning, bright eyed and bushy tailed, ready for a warm up with the rest of the cast.

JEMIMA: I'll be so bright and bushy tailed, you'll think I'm a squirrel with a couple of nuts.

RUPERT: (LOOKS WORRIED) Er...right.

JEMIMA: So that's it then, I'm reinstated.

RUPERT: Yes, you're reinstated. See you tomorrow then. Bright and early?

JEMIMA: Bright and early.

RUPERT: And then we can work on Scene 2.

JEMIMA: Er...yes Rupey, bye bye.

RUPERT: Bye, bye darling. (EXIT JEMIMA) This isn't going to work. I can feel it in my water. Where are my herbal tablets ?

(EXIT RUPERT)

SCENE 12

(ENTER LOUISE. SHE SITS DOWN WITH A PACKED LUNCH AND BEGINS TO WRITE. ENTER MR. HAINES. HE STANDS BEHIND LOUISE).

MR. HAINES: What are you doing?

LOUISE: (PANICS AND COVERS THE PAPER WITH HER HAND). It's lunchtime.

MR. HAINES: Yes, I know it's lunchtime. I asked you what you were doing, not what time it is.

LOUISE: It's private.

MR. HAINES: I bet it is.(HE GRABS THE PAPER FROM HER AND READS IT).

You're writing poetry! (LOUISE TRIES TO SNATCH THE PAPER BACK BUT HE HOLDS IT OUT OF HER REACH. WHILE HE READS IT. SHE FUMBLES WITH THE DICTOPHONE) Is this poem about me?

LOUISE: (FINALLY MANAGES TO PRESS RECORD SURREPTICIOUSLY AND TRIES TO RETRIEVE THE POEM AGAIN) It's not yours. Give it back.

MR. HAINES: It's confiscated.

LOUISE: I can do what I like during my lunch hour.

MR. HAINES: I don't like people writing poetry, especially in a working environment, especially if it's not about me. So who is it about?

LOUISE: No-one. It was just an exercise. (SHE MAKES ANOTHER GRAB FOR THE PAPER, BUT HE PULLS IT OUT OF HER REACH AGAIN)

MR. HAINES: What's the matter? Afraid that your inspiration will leave you? How can it ? Your inspiration is here...me ! No, I think I'll keep this, because deep down, I think you wrote it for me. Don't deny it? You'll only make yourself look stupid.

LOUISE: Why don't you leave me alone?

MR. HAINES: What do you mean?

LOUISE: You bully me every day.

MR. HAINES: I don't know what you mean Louise. If you didn't like me, you'd leave.

LOUISE: Why should I have to leave because of some...

MR. HAINES: Well, come on, say it. Tell me what you think of me.

LOUISE: You harass me. For example, it's lunchtime and I'm minding my own business and you've confiscated my private property.

MR. HAINES: (RETURNS THE POEM TO LOUISE) You can have your silly poem back. Your problem is, you can't take a joke. You have twenty seven minutes left on your lunch break. Don't be late. You don't want to be disciplined do you?

(EXIT MR. HAINES)

SCENE 13

(LOUISE WALKS OVER TO THE THERAPISTS SET. ENTER NORMAN, RUPERT AND BRENDA)

BRENDA: Hello everyone. How have you all got on this week? Norman?

NORMAN: I didn't make a cup of tea for Doreen when she asked. I made one for myself instead.

BRENDA: Really? What happened?

NORMAN: Doreen got very angry. She went out to meet Mr. Thomas. Perhaps I should find out where he lives and spy on him, see what he wears, how he walks, how he projects himself in his every day life. I could copy him and be a person I like for a change.

BRENDA: That's not the answer. By trying to be someone else, you're running away. You are a unique person and very valuable in your own right. Be yourself, you have a lot to offer.

NORMAN: But it's difficult.

BRENDA: It's not that difficult. You just have to keep practising until it becomes second nature.

NORMAN: What do I have to do to feel free in my own house? What do I have to do, kill her? Yes, that's an idea. I could kill her. Put something in her tea maybe?

BRENDA: No. Killing is right out Norman. Don't do any killing. That's not being very assertive at all.

RUPERT: I might be able to help.

NORMAN: Will you kill my wife?

BRENDA: Doing what?

RUPERT: Well, you know, the role playing thingy.

BRENDA: Okay Rupert. I know how keen you are to get involved in these things. So, off you go Norman, talk to your wife.

NORMAN: Er....look dear, I was thinking of going to the snooker club, would that be all right?

BRENDA: Don't ask her. Tell her.

RUPERT: Yes come on Norman, spit it out.

NORMAN: I want to...go out to play snooker.

RUPERT: Snooker ? Who put that idea into your head?

NORMAN: No-one.

RUPERT: Well someone must have. It would never come from you, you spineless little worm.

NORMAN: I...I...

RUPERT: By the way, my lover is coming round tonight, you don't mind do you?

NORMAN: What?

RUPERT: So I want you out of the house, but I'll be very annoyed if you go to that snooker hall and don't you dare go near a pub. Don't think I won't check up on you because I will.

NORMAN: Oh.

RUPERT: (BACK IN CHARACTER AS RUPERT): Well?

NORMAN: Well, what?

BRENDA: Norman, your wife is creating a sense of urgency, in order to make you tongue tied and confused, but you don't have to answer her straight away. Don't fall for the urgency ploy. Take your time, formulate an answer- and then strike!

NORMAN: Right, take my time, think, then strike.

BRENDA: You'll get used to standing up for yourself Norman, I promise. Now Louise, how did you get on in the last week?

LOUISE: Not very well. Mr. Haines wouldn't say anything incriminating when I switched on the recorder.

BRENDA: Well, there's always next time. Norman, do you think you could role play Mr. Haines, Louise's boss?

NORMAN: No, he sounds nasty. I could never be nasty.

BRENDA: What about you Rupert?

RUPERT: I think I could pull it off.

BRENDA: Now remember, you've got to play an arrogant business man. Be dominating, dogmatic and obnoxious.

RUPERT: Obnoxious ? I couldn't possibly be obnoxious.

BRENDA: Well, just pretend. Oh and try to be overbearing...if you can.

RUPERT:I'll try but I can't promise anything.

(NORMAN PUTS HIS HAND UP)

BRENDA: Yes, Norman?

NORMAN: I have to go.

BRENDA: Why?

NORMAN: I have to do the shopping and Doreen wants me back early for some strange reason.

RUPERT: Let her do the shopping on her own for a change. You only have a few hours a week of therapy and your wife is even cutting into that.

BRENDA: He's right. You need to put some time aside for yourself.

NORMAN: I know but it won't happen again. I promise. It's just this one time. She was most insistent. I have to go.

BRENDA: Very well, off you go. See you next week.

(EXIT NORMAN)

RUPERT: Are you just going to let him go?

BRENDA: I have no choice. I can't make him stand up to his wife. That's something he needs to learn to do himself. Now where were we?

RUPERT: I was going to be Mr. Haines.

BRENDA: Oh yes, now Louise, your boss is hovering suspiciously and he won't move. Rupert, stand behind her and breath on her neck or something.

(RUPERT BREATHES ON HER NECK, LIKE HE'S BREATHING ON GLASS)

BRENDA: Try to be more subtle.

LOUISE: Be a creep.

RUPERT: Well, I'm not sure if I can be one of those people. I must say this man sounds awful. I would like to beat him up for you darling. In fact, I will do when I see him.

BRENDA: Okay, now, let's concentrate. Louise, Mr. Haines is behind you and he's breathing down your neck, like so. (RUPERT PUTS HIS HANDS ON LOUISE'S SHOULDERS) Now they're on your hips, now moving down to.... (LOUISE BREAKS AWAY FROM RUPERT) Rupert, I asked you to pretend.

RUPERT: I was pretending. I was pretending to be a creep.

BRENDA: Are you comfortable with this Louise? We can stop any time you want to.

LOUISE: No, it's okay. He did the right thing. I almost turned round and slapped him.

RUPERT: Oh dear, I'm glad you didn't.

LOUISE: But it made me feel good that I might do it. I didn't freeze when Rupert touched me. I didn't go cold.

RUPERT: Well, I do have that effect on women.

LOUISE: I really felt in control that time, but perhaps that was because it was with Rupert and not Mr. Haines.

BRENDA: Now this time, I want you to show your feelings. Don't hold back. Get angry.

LOUISE: I don't want to make a scene.

BRENDA: Make a scene and enjoy making a scene.

LOUISE: Okay, I'll try.

BRENDA: Off you go Rupert. Molest at will!

RUPERT: (CLEARS THROAT) Er...Louise, you've got a great bottom.

(HE LIGHTLY TOUCHES HER BOTTOM. SHE TURNS AND DOES A MARTIAL ART MOVE ON HIM. HE ENDS UP ON HIS BACK, ON THE FLOOR).

LOUISE: I'm sorry Rupert.

BRENDA: What did you do?

LOUISE: I did a course once in ju-jitsu. I left after a few weeks. That's the only throw I learned. (RUPERT GROANS) I honestly don't know where that came from. I didn't think I had it in me.

BRENDA: Violence is not the answer Louise, but self defence is very assertive. You were just protecting yourself. There's nothing wrong with that.

LOUISE: Rupert, you're not hurt are you? (LOUISE AND BRENDA HELP HIM TO HIS FEET).

RUPERT: There doesn't seem to be any broken bones. Don't worry, it's not your fault. I shouldn't have touched your bottom.

LOUISE: That's all right. I think I'm going to feel a bit more confident facing Mr. Haines now.

BRENDA: Good, and what about you Rupert? How are you getting on with Jemima?

RUPERT: I've had some positive moments. Jemima begged me for her job back...and I very deliberately took my time reinstating her.

BRENDA: But Rupert, that puts you in the same position as you were in before.

RUPERT: I suppose so.

BRENDA: Since it seems to be Jemima's brother who is holding all the power regarding the play, why don't you speak to him? Tell him about the problems you've been having with Jemima.

RUPERT: Oh, I couldn't do that.

BRENDA: Why not?

RUPERT: Well because, he'll be offended.

BRENDA: Do you know him well enough to know that he would be offended?

RUPERT: Well actually no, but I'm imagining that he might be. I don't want to lose my job as a director.

BRENDA: But it's better than the stress you are going through now. I have one word to say to you Rupert. (PAUSE) Flop.

RUPERT: Flop?

BRENDA: And who gets the blame when a play is a flop?

BRENDA and RUPERT and LOUISE: (ALL TOGETHER): The director.

BRENDA: And remember those other four words...'Director of the year?'
RUPERT: Yes.
BRENDA: I can almost see it in neon lights.
RUPERT: Yes!
BRENDA: Next to your name.
RUPERT: Oh yes!
BRENDA: So? Rupert?
RUPERT: (SNAPS OUT OF IT): Okay, I'll phone him now. (HE DIALS HIS MOBILE): Er...hello Howard. How are you? Yes, I'm fine. I'm just calling to say....that...erm....that...(LOUISE & BRENDA ENCOURAGE HIM TO SPEAK UP) What was that? Jemima? Oh yes Howard, she's fabulous. (COLLECTIVE GROANS FROM BRENDA AND LOUISE) Yes, no problems there. She's one of the best. Yes. I'm very much looking forward to opening night. Yes. Okay, goodbye. Yes, same to you. Bye. (ENDS CALL. BRENDA AND LOUISE STARE HARD AT HIM).Yes, yes, I know. I messed up.
BRENDA: You're going to call him right back, right now.
RUPERT: No.
BRENDA: Yes. (GRABS THE PHONE FROM HIM) This does have redial doesn't it?
RUPERT: No, no!
BRENDA: (PRESSES REDIAL): It's ringing. (HANDS PHONE TO RUPERT)
RUPERT: Hello Howard. It's Rupert again. I haven't been completely honest with you. I'm having a problem with one of the actors. Yes, she's just not right for the part. She's not turning up for rehearsal. She's completely unreliable and putting the play in jeopardy. (PAUSE) Oh, er...Jemima. (PAUSE) Really? Yes, I suppose you're right, I am the director! Thank you very much Howard. Bye. (ENDS CALL)
BRENDA and LOUISE: Well?
RUPERT: He said that he knows how difficult Jemima can be and they fight like cat and dog all the time. The bottom line is... if she's causing problems, then it's fine by him if I replace her.
BRENDA: That's wonderful news Rupert. Well done.
LOUISE: Yes, that was very assertive of you.
RUPERT: I feel much better now. You were right Brenda.
BRENDA: Well, I am right occasionally. Come on, let's celebrate with a nice cup of tea.
LOUISE: Coffee for me.

RUPERT: And a nice digestive biscuit. (PUTS HIS HANDS ON HIS BACK) Ah !
BRENDA: Are you all okay?
RUPERT: Just a twinge.
(EXIT BRENDA, RUPERT AND LOUISE)

SCENE 14

(ENTER NORMAN AND DOREEN)

DOREEN: Now look Norman, I'm going away for the weekend.
NORMAN: Who with?
DOREEN: A friend.
NORMAN: Mr. Thomas?
DOREEN: It's none of your business.
NORMAN: It is my business. I'm your husband.
DOREEN: While I'm away I want you to re-decorate the kitchen.
NORMAN: It doesn't need re-decorating.
DOREEN: Yes, it does.
NORMAN: I'm not doing it.
DOREEN: Yes, you are and I need some money.
NORMAN: I don't have any. You can search me if you want.
DOREEN: Now don't be silly.
NORMAN: I just told you Doreen, I don't have any. You took it all the other day and before you ask, I don't have a bank card on me either.
DOREEN: What has got into you Norman?
NORMAN: What has got into me, is, the realisation that we are over.
DOREEN: What are you talking about? You are going to give me some money and I'm going to go away and while I'm away you're going to redecorate the kitchen.
NORMAN: what happened to us Doreen?
DOREEN: What do you mean?
NORMAN: We used to be so happy.
DOREEN: Well...not any more.
NORMAN: Don't you remember our wedding day?
DOREEN: I remember it rained.
NORMAN: But we were happy and in love.
DOREEN: People change. I've changed.
NORMAN: You don't need to tell me that.
DOREEN: Well, I'm off. See you Sunday night. (SHE IS ABOUT TO EXIT BUT THERE IS SOMEONE AT THE DOOR. ENTER BRENDA)
BRENDA: Is Norman there please?
DOREEN: Who are you?
BRENDA: Ah, hello Norman, I just came to tell you the next meeting is on Tuesday and not Monday next week. I was able to contact the others by

phone but I couldn't get through to you.

DOREEN: So this what you've been getting up to?

BRENDA: I beg your pardon?

DOREEN: This is what you've been doing, having an affair behind my back.

Brenda: so this is Doreen. My confidentiality policy forbids me to say what I want to say next.

NORMAN: Hypocrite.

DOREEN: Who is this woman Norman? You'd better talk fast or you're in big trouble, that is, bigger trouble than what you were in a second ago.

NORMAN: Well, you see dear, I've been on a course to help me er....be assertive.

DOREEN: What are you talking about? Have you lost your mind? You, going on a course to be assertive. I've never heard anything so ridiculous in all my life.

NORMAN: Yes, it is ridiculous. Who did I think I was? All I wanted was a little kindness and self respect...but I don't deserve it do I? But I can still show you what I've learned. You're quite right. I am having an affair with this woman.

DOREEN and BRENDA: What?

NORMAN: You heard.

DOREEN:I knew it.

NORMAN: Yes, I' having a torrid affair. This woman makes me feel like a man. This woman is warm, soft, pliable...

DOREEN: I want a divorce.

NORMAN: No, I want a divorce.

DOREEN: I said it first.

NORMAN: I was thinking it first, so there.

DOREEN: I'm keeping the house.

NORMAN: It was my mothers and it's in my name remember? I'll be changing the locks so don't expect to get in on Sunday night.

DOREEN: But what will I do? Where will I live?

NORMAN: Why don't you go and live with Mr. Thomas?

DOREEN: He's married.

NORMAN: Oh well, looks like it's back to mother. (EXIT DOREEN) I'm free! I'm free! It feels so good!

BRENDA: Lies are not assertive Norman. They're manipulative.

NORMAN: Sorry.

BRENDA: Why did you say we were having an affair?

NORMAN: I don't know. I just felt like it. I wanted her to feel the same pain she gave me. You helped me stand up to her. Do you think I've changed?

BRENDA: Yes I do.

NORMAN: Am I taller, more attractive?

BRENDA: You know, you do seem to have grown.

NORMAN: Am I more assertive?

BRENDA: Yes.

NORMAN : Would you like to have a cup of tea while I call the locksmith?

BRENDA: It would be a pleasure.

(EXIT BRENDA AND NORMAN)

SCENE 15

(ENTER RUPERT AND JEMIMA)

JEMIMA: Why did you tell Howard you were having problems with me?

RUPERT: Oh...er...I was going to tell you. I mean, explain to you...

JEMIMA: But you didn't.

RUPERT: But I'm doing it now. In order to be an actor you have to be responsible and reliable, not just talented.

JEMIMA: Don't beat about the bush Rupey, tell me the truth.

RUPERT: I've just told you. You agreed that you would come in early every morning etc. and it hasn't happened. I can't trust you...and I can't have you in this play.

JEMIMA: Won't is the word Rupert. You won't have me in this play. You'll ruin me if you sack me. Please have mercy.

RUPERT: No, this time I won't take you back.

JEMIMA: But acting is my whole life. I admit that I'm having a few teeny weeny problems at the moment.

RUPERT: Teeny weeny?

JEMIMA: But haven't we worked well together in the past Rupey? Haven't we had some success together?

RUPERT; Some, but...

JEMIMA: I can't work with anyone but you. We're like salt and pepper together, like strawberries and cream.

RUPERT: Well, I...

JEMIMA: Oh Rupey, things will never be the same without you. You're such a wonderful director and I'd hate us to part like this. I know you feel the same.

RUPERT: Well, I don't know. I've...made my decision. I think I should stick with it.

JEMIMA: Who's taking my place?

RUPERT: Hannah.

JEMIMA: She couldn't act her way out of a paper bag and she couldn't possibly play Elizabeth. She doesn't have the sexual presence.

RUPERT: I admit. She wasn't my first choice.

JEMIMA: Well there you go you see. Oh Rupey, please give me one more chance, just one more chance.

RUPERT: (SIGHS) Oh, all right then.

JEMIMA: Is that it then? You're giving me my job back?

RUPERT: Yes, yes. I suppose I am.

JEMIMA: Good, because now I can tell you what to do with your stinking job. I resign.

RUPERT: What?

JEMIMA: You're a bad director Rupert. In fact, I think you're the pits and I've got better things to do with my time.

RUPERT: You really are a cruel little...

JEMIMA: Go on – say it ! You've never had any backbone have you? Not even to tell me what you think of me. How can someone like you demand respect?

RUPERT: What makes you think anyone else is going to employ you as an actress ?

JEMIMA: I have my ways.

RUPERT: And lying on your back is one of them.

JEMIMA: I beg your pardon. I've never had to use the casting couch in my life.

RUPERT: Well, there's a first time for everything isn't there?

JEMIMA: How dare you.

RUPERT: You're fired.

JEMIMA: How can I be fired. I've just resigned.

RUPERT: But I've just fired you.

JEMIMA: No, I resigned before you fired me.

RUPERT: No, I fired you-then you resigned and now I'm firing you again.

JEMIMA: Oh no you're not.

RUPERT: Oh yes I am.

JEMIMA: Right, that's enough. I resign!

RUPERT: No, I fired you! I fired you! (EXIT JEMIMA) Jemima, you're as wooden as a tree..Do you hear me? You're as hammy as a pig. At least have the decency to stay here while I'm putting you down! (EXIT RUPERT)

SCENE 16

(ENTER MR. HAINES WHO SITS DOWN AT HIS DESK AND STARTS. WRITING. ENTER LOUISE)

LOUISE: You wanted to see me?

MR. HAINES: Yes. Take a seat. (SHE SITS DOWN AND STARTS THE RECORING DEVICE) Louise, I'm afraid I have to let you go.

LOUISE: What?

MR. HAINES: You haven't been working here for very long. Although that's not the reason I'm firing you.

LOUISE: The reason you're firing me is because I haven't been very nice to you.

MR. HAINES: You don't know me at all Louise. You see, this is why I want us to have dinner together or something, just so we can get to know each other, just so all of these misunderstandings can be avoided.

LOUISE: I'd rather not if you don't mind. I mean, I respect you as my boss, but that's as far as it goes.

MR. HAINES: I see, but it doesn't really matter. I'm letting you go nevertheless.

LOUISE: And your reason for firing me would be?

MR. HAINES: Oh that's easy- incompatible personalities.

LOUISE: I don't think that's a sack-able offence. Incompatible means you're firing me because I won't go out with you, I won't be 'nice' to you and we all know what that means. I wonder what Mr. Johnson would say if I told him that you scuppered my promotion?

MR. HAINES: I already explained that to you Louise. People skills. You don't have them.

LOUISE: I'm good with people and you know it. Mr. Johnson knows it.

MR. HAINES: Maybe but he's an idiot. He'll believe anything I say. Got him wrapped around my little finger.

LOUISE: Really?

MR. HAINES: It should be me on the second floor, not him. He wouldn't recognise a good employee if it bit him on the nose, but I do Louise. I appreciate you. You just don't appreciate me.

LOUISE: You told me my work was faultless.

MR. HAINES: It is.

LOUISE: You said I was a good worker, a model employee.

MR. HAINES: You are.

LOUISE: Could you say that again, a bit louder?

MR.HAINES: No. There's nothing more to say Louise. It's dinner or the dole.

(EXIT LOUISE. EXIT MR. HAINES)

SCENE 17

(ENTER BRENDA. ENTER RUPERT)

RUPERT: I have some good news. I fired Jemima.

BRENDA: Well done Rupert. You should have told me you were going to do that. We could have role played.

RUPERT: I thought I would bottle out if I had to rehearse it.

BRENDA: The idea is that by rehearsing you don't bottle out. So what happened exactly?

RUPERT: First she resigned, as you know, then I took her back. Today I fired her, then she resigned and I fired her again.

BRENDA: That's very assertive of you Rupert.

(ENTER LOUISE)

BRENDA: Hello Louise.

RUPERT: Hello Louise. Have you done any acting?

LOUISE: No.

BRENDA: Rupert, don't you have a replacement for Jemima?

RUPERT: I always thought it would be insulting to have an understudy for her. I never thought she would let me down. I let her think that I'd asked Hannah to replace her, but I haven't asked anyone yet.

BRENDA: You don't face reality Rupert. That's your problem.

RUPERT: Well that and the fact that I'm a bad director.

BRENDA: But you won't be from now on will you?

RUPERT: True, true. Louise, will you be in the play I'm directing? I think you'll suit the part. All you have to do is learn a couple of lines.

BRENDA: A couple?

RUPERT: Ssshhh !

LOUISE: I've never been on stage before but I'll have a go.

RUPERT: Oh, it's easy, once you get the hang of it.

BRENDA: But Rupert...

RUPERT: Shush please Brenda. Now Louise, can you say 'Your dinner's in the dog'? Say it.

LOUISE: Your dinner's in the dog.

RUPERT: Oh brilliant, fantastic.

BRENDA: She already has a job.

LOUISE: Well, actually...not any more.

(ENTER NORMAN)

BRENDA: Hello Norman.

RUPERT: Hello Norman. Pull up a chair old chap. So, will you be in the play Louise?

BRENDA: Wait a minute. Louise, what's all this about you not having a job any more?

LOUISE: I was sacked yesterday but I've recorded Mr. Haines saying some things about his boss and some other incriminating stuff regarding me.

NORMAN: You should make a copy of it.

LOUISE: I made several copies. The only problem I have now is confronting him with the evidence.

NORMAN: Oh, I'll come with you Louise. I'll stick it to him.

BRENDA: Steady on Norman, you need to wear in those new assertive shoes of yours.

NORMAN: No. I'm fine. I'm good at this now.

BRENDA: What happened after you changed the locks?

Norman: oh Doreen's back at her mother's. I'm watching lots of snooker and making lots of friends at the snooker hall.

BRENDA: Well done Norman. We're really proud of you.

LOUISE: What have you done Norman?

RUPERT: Did you stand up to your wife?

NORMAN: Yes. You are now looking at a new man.

RUPERT: Is it a plane ? Is it a bird? No, it's Assertive Man!

LOUISE: Is that what happens when you finish this course, you become a superhero ?

BRENDA: Yes.

RUPERT: Oh well, I'm a superhero then. That's if Louise decides to do the play.

LOUISE: Okay. I'll do the play.

RUPERT: Thank you.

LOUISE: No problem.

BRENDA: Are you sure Louise?

LOUISE: I quite fancy the whole acting thing. It's something I've always wanted to do.

BRENDA: So what happens now? Are you going to confront Mr. Haines?

LOUISE: Yes.

BRENDA: When ?

LOUISE: After I leave here, I suppose. I'm dreading it.

NORMAN: We'll come with you!

RUPERT: Yes, we'll support you.

BRENDA: You mean we all just gang up on him?

RUPERT: Yes, why not?

BRENDA: I think in normal circumstances, we should keep in mind that the other person involved has rights too...but I think we'll overlook it this time.

NORMAN: Good. Well come on, let's go.

LOUISE: Wait. Why don't I just bypass Mr. Haines and take the tape to Mr. Johnson on the second floor ? I'm sure that would do the trick.

RUPERT: But that wouldn't be as much fun darling.

NORMAN: No, it wouldn't.

BRENDA: No, it wouldn't. Let's go.

(EXIT BRENDA, RUPERT, NORMAN AND LOUISE)

SCENE 18

(ENTER MR. HAINES. HE SITS DOWN AND STARTS TO WRITE. ENTER LOUISE)

MR. HAINES: Don't you knock any more?

LOUISE: I don't work here any more.

MR.HAINES: Oh yes, well, if you've got something to say, then say it. If not, then clear out your desk, say goodbye to your colleagues and get out.

LOUISE: Well actually, I have got something to say...I've been thinking...

MR. HAINES: How unusual for you. (PAUSE) Well? What's the matter, cat got your tongue?

LOUISE: Remember when you ripped up that application form in front of me?

MR. HAINES: Yes I do actually. I still smile when I think of it.

LOUISE: Well I'm glad you feel like that because I have a small recording device hidden about my person and I've been recording every conversation we've been having for the past week. (MR. HAINES LAUGHS) What's so funny?

MR. HAINES: You are Louise. Do you expect me to believe that?

LOUISE: No, I don't. It's your privilege not to believe me now, but as soon as I give the tape to Mr. Johnson, then you'll have no choice but to believe.

MR. HAINES: You're not serious ? You couldn't be, not you. I think you're bluffing. You wouldn't have the guts to complain to Mr. Johnson, otherwise you'd have done it by now.

LOUISE: I will go to see him. I'm recording this conversation now.

MR.HAINES: And you have a something hidden about your person do you? (HE STANDS UP AND MOVES TOWARDS HER) Let's prove it.

LOUISE: I don't have to prove anything to you but here's a tape. (SHE SHOWS HIM THE RECORDER AND TAKES OUT THE TAPE. HE SNATCHES IT FROM HER AND EXPENDS A LOT OF ENERGY DESTROYING IT) I do have three more copies.

MR. HAINES: (MOVES TOWARDS HER MENACINGLY) Once a mouse, always a mouse.

LOUISE: (BACKS AWAY AND CRIES OUT) Norman!

(ENTER NORMAN, RUPERT AND BRENDA)

NORMAN: Now you have a few more mice to contend with.

MR. HAINES: Who are you?

Norman: They're my friends.

MR. HAINES: Friends ? You ? Don't make me laugh. Whoever you all are, you need to leave this office now. I'll give you five seconds to get out and then I'm calling security. 1...2...3...4...

(ENTER DOREEN)

DOREEN: Peter...

MR. HAINES: Doreen!

NORMAN: DOREEN?

DOREEN: Norman.

NORMAN: Peter?

DOREEN: (WALKS OVER TO MR. HAINES) Mr. Thomas.

NORMAN: Mr. Thomas?

LOUISE: But your name is Mr. Haines.

MR. HAINES: Well, I have a number of aliases. I am a married man you know. I have to be careful.

NORMAN: So let me get this straight ? You're Mr. Thomas, the man who's been having an affair with my wife?

MR. HAINES: A bit.

NORMAN: A bit?

DOREEN: And this is the woman you've been having an affair with?

BRENDA: No. I am not having an affair with Norman. He was just making that all up.

(NORMAN WALKS MENACINGLY TOWARDS MR. HAINES).

MR. HAINES: Now, let's not be hasty.

NORMAN: (STALKS MR. HAINES AROUND THE STAGE) Rupert, get him.

(RUPERT AMBUSHES MR. HAINES AND HOLDS HIM STILL UNTIL NORMAN GETS TO HIM). This is for your long suffering wife.(POKES HIM IN THE EYE) This is for DOREEN.(STAMPS ON HIS FOOT) And this is for Louise.(KNEES HIM IN THE GROIN).And now I'm going to phone your wife.

MR. HAINES: No, no please.

NORMAN: Well then, will Louise get her job back?

MR. HAINES: Yes, yes.

BRENDA: And will she be allowed her promotion to the second floor?

MR. HAINES: Yes, yes, only please don't tell my wife.

DOREEN: (HELPS MR. HAINES OFF THE STAGE) Come on, I'll make you a nice cup of tea. (EXIT DOREEN AND MR. HAINES)

RUPERT: Well that was interesting.

BRENDA: Yes, nothing like a spot of blackmail when assertiveness won't do.

LOUISE: Thanks everyone. Norman you were amazing.

NORMAN: Oh, it was nothing.

RUPERT: I don't know about anyone else but I could do with a nice cup of tea after all that fighting.

NORMAN: Me too.

RUPERT: Well come on, Norman, make the tea.

NORMAN: Oh stop it. Stop it. That doesn't work on me any more.

BRENDA: I'll make the tea, a celebratory tea. (EXIT BRENDA AND NORMAN)

RUPERT: Now that you've got your job back, will you still be in my show?

LOUISE: Yes, of course. I'll rehearse in the evenings.

RUPERT: Thank you. Director of the year, here I come!

(EXIT RUPERT AND LOUISE)

CURTAIN